Retirement Planning

This material is educational in nature and should not be deemed as a solicitation of any specific product or service. All investments involve risk and a potential loss of principal. Kalos Capital nor Kalos Management offer tax and legal advice. Please consult with a tax advisor or attorney for advice regarding the impact on your portfolio.
Securities offered through Kalos Capital, Inc. and Investment advisory services offered through Kalos Management, Inc. located at 11525 Park Wood Circle, Alpharetta, GA 30005. Skrobonja Financial Group is not a subsidiary of Kalos Capital, Inc. nor Kalos Management, Inc.
Please note that the presenter can provide information, but not give tax or Social Security advice. Consumers should seek guidance from their tax advisor or the Social Security Administration regarding their particular situation. The presenter may be able to identify potential retirement income gaps and may introduce insurance products, such as a fixed annuity, as a potential solution. Not approved by, endorsed by, or affiliated with the U.S. Government or any governmental agency..

Printed by:
90-Minute Books
302 Martinique Drive
Winter Haven, FL 33884
www.90minutebooks.com

For more information on 90-Minute Books including finding out how you can publish your own book, visit 90minutebooks.com or call (863) 318-0464

Here's What's Inside…

Retirement Planning!

When I talk about my definition of retirement, I think it sometimes catches people off guard. In my mind, retirement is not who you are or where you're at in life, rather it's the transition of your time and money. In other words, it is a process you go through… not your identity.

The transition of *money* is a transition from accumulating money to using it. For *time*, it is a transition of reallocating the 40-plus hours per week you spent working.

However, when I meet with new clients to discuss their retirement goals, regardless of how much money they have saved or experience they have investing, they're often a little confused, or even anxious, about their options. In fact, many retirees are simply at a loss when it comes to understanding what steps to take to experience a smooth retirement transition. The reason? Living a life of purpose and abundance in retirement requires a shift in mindset.

New retirees need to bridge the gap between what they dream about in their thinking time and what they need to do with their money to make their dreams a reality.

But without knowing how to go about this, people will inherently default to what they know and think they understand — which, when it comes to making financial decisions, is most often rates of return and account balances.

As a result, retirees experience disconnect between what they see as the purpose for their money and what their money is actually doing for them.

When you transition to retirement, you have an opportunity to do all those things with your money that you've been dreaming about during your working years. But to do so, you'll have to shift your mindset about money from one focused on accumulating more to one focused on actually using it and putting your savings toward all those things that will allow you to live a life of purpose in retirement.

In this book, I share my thoughts on retirement planning, so readers can better understand that it's okay to use their money. My philosophy for retirement planning is that the whole purpose of saving money is to be able to access and use it when you need it. So let's use it!

I hope this book helps you better understand how to use your money to live your life to the fullest in retirement. If you have goals and dreams, whether that's traveling, building a second home, paying for your kids' college education, or starting a new business, let's put a plan in place to make those dreams happen!

To Your Success!

Stock Broker or Retirement Planner?

Time and time again I hear from retirees who are stressed about how to get organized and prepared for retirement. They're not sure where to turn for guidance, leaving them ill-prepared for what is before them.

What's puzzling to me is that most people who come into my office have stock brokers who they have used for years—in some cases, even decades. In other words, they have had financial professionals in their lives, yet no retirement planning or preparation has been done.

Why is this happening?

In my many years of working with clients, I have found there is a misconception that a stock broker has your entire financial picture in mind when they make investment recommendations. However, this is not necessarily true. What's important to remember is that having a stock broker and an investment portfolio isn't the same as having a retirement plan.

Therefore, a stock broker isn't likely to talk with you about the details of your retirement. A stock broker is trained to invest your money, and that is what they do. Their primary focus is, and will always be, accumulation.

This may be fine for you while you're still working because you're living off your earned income, but when you retire, reality hits. Now, the dollars you have saved become much more important because your needs have changed.

But more than likely, your stock broker won't shift their strategies. They'll want to continue with the status quo of growing your money for the future. This disconnect can, understandably, be very frustrating and confusing.

Alleviating this frustration and confusion is really quite simple when you accept that growing money is done one way while distributing income is done another way.

When you are accumulating money, you often seek stock market returns with the hope that over the years—after the ups and downs—you have made more than you have lost. On the other hand, when you retire, the focus should switch to distribution and preservation.

When it comes to retirement, many of the designs and strategies I help clients with are utilization strategies. I realize people don't save money just to have money. They save money to use it when they need it.

However, changing your mindset so that you feel comfortable going against your stock broker's advice and actually using your money isn't easy. That's why taking time to create a retirement plan focused on adjusting and solidifying your money mindsets, addressing what you can control, and protecting yourself from what you can't is essential. More on that in the next chapter.

Retirement Mindsets

The older I get the more I realize the impact our mindsets have on every aspect of our life, including our finances. Your mindsets–what you think about, what you believe, and the way you go about making decisions and living life– are a direct result of how you think. This is a very powerful thing to understand about yourself, and I hope you allow me the opportunity to explain why this has everything to do with your money and your future.

We all know that there is no shortage of information and opinions on the topic of money. Turn on the TV and you are inundated with commercials for products, services, books, and seminars that are screaming for your attention. Meanwhile, we read blogs, listen to podcasts, and hear friends and family discuss things we should and shouldn't do with money.

On a daily basis, we have to process an overwhelming amount of content that seems impossible to sort through and understand. In fact, it is said that the brain processes 400 billion bits of information per second, and it is estimated that we actually consume 34 gigabits of information per day. The result is that our brains are set to overdrive trying to sort through and make sense of what we are consuming.

To cope, our brains seek short cuts by trying to connect new information with something we are already familiar with; similar to how an assembly line grabs things and sorts them into predefined categories. This process reduces the amount of thought that goes into figuring out what something means.

It is only when something comes along that we cannot categorize that we pause and seek just enough additional information so that our brains can get it sorted as quickly as possible. The challenge is that once you have created this association or pathway in your mind about something, it is difficult to redefine it unless you stop to consider what is happening.

This is why when it comes to money, people tend to lump much of what they think they know into a mental file with a "dollar sign" on it and anything that has a dollar sign associated with it gets thrown into that mental file. In reality, the file ends up being more like a mental junk drawer full of mismatched information.

The take away from all of this is that a lot of what you hear about money may seem like it is all similar since it has a dollar sign attached to it, but it really isn't. Unless you take the time to understand what you are consuming, you run the risk of making mistakes and missing opportunities.

Especially when it comes to your money, you shouldn't be so quick to judge and assume you already know everything. Relying too much on what you think you know and not taking the time to challenge your thinking is just a bad idea. To achieve financial freedom and live a life of abundance, you need to avoid being trapped in a bubble of your current thoughts and beliefs. You need to raise your curiosity flag and begin asking questions. There are four important points to think about here:

- You'll never know everything so don't assume you do.

- Avoid sacred cows in your mindset. Things change and so should you.

- Remove limiting beliefs that prevent you from believing things that really are possible.

- Remain curious and challenge why you believe what you believe to avoid hanging on to things you may believe are true but that are actually false.

When you begin to open up to learning more, being curious, and challenging what you believe, you can start to develop mindsets rooted in facts that will guide your financial progress.

So, how do you begin to challenge your old mindsets about money, financial planning, and retirement? The first thing is to stop and think. We think all the time, but the average thought is rooted in fear and insecurity. If we allow it, our thoughts will wander endlessly with no destination. If this is the majority of your thinking, there's no progress being made.

We need to develop our creative thinking. Think about what you believe and ask yourself why you believe it. Think about your goals so that you can strategically move closer to them. You can think of this process as cleaning out your mental junk drawer. When you clean out a junk drawer, you throw more than half of the stuff away and wonder why you ever hung on to it in the first place. You also get a sense of satisfaction and organization.

You can apply this to how you think about money by writing down all of your beliefs about money–everything that you've read, everything you've been told, everything you've heard other people saying, all the things you've held onto as truth. Completing this exercise will help you clean out your mental junk drawer and help you build organized and meaningful mindsets about money.

These ideas you're hanging onto are driving your behavior. So, once you have your list, begin to ask questions and challenge why you believe what you believe. Simply ask "Why?" to each of the ideas you have written down. Then, ask yourself if the ideas have been tested or if they are just concepts? Is it something that just sounds right or is it something where the math has been shown to support the claim?

The media, columnists, and financial entertainers are constantly spreading concepts and ideas about things. A lot of these things get floated around as truth but have never been truly tested. Now is the time to test the ideas you have that are formulating your mindsets around money.

Once you've sorted through and organized the ideas and beliefs about money that serve a purpose for you and have discarded those that don't, the next step is to begin to change any outdated or ineffective mindsets you have about money. To do so, you'll need to address what I think is at the root of all financial planning decisions–defining the intention you have for your money.

Here's a helpful exercise that can help you do that. Imagine you have an additional $100/mo. How much would that change your life? What could you do if you had that extra income?

Now, imagine you have an additional $1,000/mo. How much would that change your life? What could you do if you had that extra income?

Now, ask the same questions about increasingly higher levels of monthly income. How would your life change and what could you do with an extra $10,000/month, $100,000/month, and $1,000,000/month?

Most likely, these income escalations had you visualizing a more secure life as the numbers grew larger. Reflecting back to your thoughts throughout this exercise, at what monthly amount, did you stop thinking about yourself and start thinking about helping other people, your family, friends, charities? What was that number for you? Was it $100, $10,000, $100,000, $1,000,000?

Here is what is happening when you think about money in this manner: you're focusing on what actually matters in your financial life. What limits your ability to retire, to give, to help others is the absence of financial security. In the absence of financial security, there is no confidence. You probably have retirement assets, you probably have money saved somewhere, but what's missing and preventing connecting your money with your highest intentions for your money is that security of income.

To achieve security of income, you have to break out of status quo mindsets that are limiting what you can do with your money. You can't be complacent. You have to be willing to open your way of thinking to the following three essential mindset shifts. These mindset shifts will help you achieve security of income so that you can live a life of abundance in retirement:

1) Reframe Your Mindset about Money. I think aligning your money with your purpose is so important that I dedicated my podcast, "Common Sense Financial Podcast", to that message. Too often, I find that people, especially new retirees, think their money is aligned with their purpose only to find that their money is actually sitting in a 401(k) or IRA where its #1 purpose is growth or they have large amounts of cash just sitting there doing nothing for them at all.

With each episode of my podcast, my goal is to help my listeners bridge the gap between their hopes and dreams and what they can do with their money to make those hopes and dreams a reality. Too often the default position people take when it comes to their money is ensuring high rates of return and bolstering account balances–simply because that's what they think they know and understand about money.

The reality is you need to reframe your mindset about money. Instead of focusing on rates of return and how much money is in your accounts, the focus should be on how much income you can generate from your assets. By focusing on how much income your assets are generating, you have a true measurement of how close you are to achieving financial freedom status and the ability to give and contribute to those around you. As a result, you'll experience the financial freedom that will allow you to turn the hopes and dreams you have for your money—your money's true purpose—into a reality.

2) Reframe Your Mindset of Time. In his coaching program, Strategic Coach®, Dan Sullivan has an exercise called The Lifetime Extender®. It's a great way to reframe how you think about time. Basically, it asks that you adjust your timeframe. For example, instead of thinking about retirement as the final portion of your life, imagine you have a whole other lifetime ahead of you. For example, Dan's timeframe has him living to 156!

What this exercise helps us do is stop thinking of retirement as an end point. When it simply becomes the transition point to another long section of your life you can expand your focus. You can expand your purpose. Instead of thinking about how you'll fill your time in your final years, you can start to think about how you'll fulfill your purpose in the days, weeks, and years ahead.

3) Reinvent Yourself. There's a book I love called *Halftime* Bob Buford. Buford illustrates the theme that wherever you are in your life right now is your "halftime." And with that knowledge, you should take steps to make the next half of your life the better half.

When you retire, you're coming out of decades of dedicating yourself to your career. There's a chance you spent more time at your job with your coworkers and/or your clients than you did at home with your family. It's very likely that the level of dedication you made to your career developed into a sense of purpose. But when you retire, all of that goes away. Suddenly, there's a void, and you may end up feeling lost, unfulfilled, and even depressed.

This aspect of transitioning into retirement is why I always ask my clients to consider how they'll be spending their time in retirement. Sure, this is essential knowledge for us for cash flow planning purposes, but more importantly, it gets them thinking about what their purpose will be in the next half of their life. Retirement is an opportunity to reinvent yourself, to leave your pre-retirement self behind, and find new purpose in this next phase of your life.

I often hear people describe themselves as "retired." I think that label is troubling because usually when we think of something as being "retired" the connotation is that it has outlived its usefulness. But when you retire, your life's purpose doesn't cease. You still have many years ahead to fulfill your purpose, refine your talents, and create wonderful experiences.

I invite you to think of retirement not as a label or an identity but as a transition. When you shift your mindsets about retirement, your money, and your time, you can begin to live a life of abundance.

Investing for Financial Freedom

Most of the average person's investments are tied directly to the stock market. But watching your money rise and fall with the ups and downs of the stock market is what I call a spectator approach to money. All you can do is sit back and watch to see what happens, entirely focused on your rate of return, with no real control over the outcome. For many average investors, this approach leads to frustration, disappointment, and disillusion.

OK, you might be thinking, *then, where should I be investing my money?* Well, if I was simply trying to sell books, I'd insert a one-size-fits-all answer right here. But it's not that simple. Every investor operates with varying degrees of resources, knowledge, and experience – and we all have different tolerances when it comes to one key factor–risk.

For some people, the idea of making 10% or losing 10% of their portfolio is really not a big deal. For others, this would be unimaginable.

So the idea of giving blanket advice to everyone without considering risk tolerance would be irresponsible.

In other words, how you view your money will often determine the amount of risk you're willing to take, which in turn can help define what type of investments to consider. To learn what level of risk you're willing to accept, find out your Risk Score at **getyourfreeriskscore.com.**

Once you have your Risk Score, you can use it to better assess how to use your money. Throughout the rest of this chapter, I'll be covering 401(k)s and pensions, which are where most people traditionally have their money accumulated as they go into retirement. We'll also take a closer look at life insurance, annuities, and private investments as conduits for using your accumulated money to generate more income.

401(k)s and Pensions

When developing your retirement plan, it's very likely that one part of that process will be determining how to allocate funds from either a 401(k) or a pension.

Generally, I'm not a fan of 401(k)s or pensions. I think they require you to give up too much control over your money for too long. But that said, a big benefit of these retirement saving options is that they're easy to contribute to, and in the case of 401(k)s, your employer may even offer a match that boosts your contributions.

I would never recommend that these accounts be your sole method of saving for retirement, but because so many people have one or the other of these (or in some cases, both), I do think it's important to take a look at how you can organize that money to make it work for you and help those funds fulfill their purpose.

First, let's look at 401(k)s:

Let's say that hypothetically you have $500,000 sitting in a 401(k) at work. Let's also assume you need $4,000 a month to live on. When you get ready to retire, $2,500 a month will be fulfilled through Social Security, leaving a $1,500 deficit per month.

How much of your $500,000 needs to be designated for income, and how much should be stored for a future purpose? To determine this, you take your $1,500 monthly deficit and multiply it by 12 months. That shows you that you need $18,000 a year from this asset.

There are different distribution rates we can assume: 4%, 5%, or 6%. Let's say we're shooting for a 5% distribution rate. If you take the $18,000 and divide your 5% distribution rate into it, it means we need a principal amount of $360,000. Therefore, $360,000 of the $500,000 sitting in your retirement account would be earmarked for income. We would take that $360,000 and shoot for a 5% distribution rate, which gives you $18,000 a year or $1,500 a month, filling the gap in your budget.

Often, when people are working, they think, "I have money leftover at the end of the month! I'm pretty comfortable; I don't need to be tracking or planning things." What I hope the above example shows is that when you hit retirement, it becomes more and more critical to get in tune with what your specific needs are. Otherwise, your assets could be mishandled, and you don't want to do that when you're looking at potentially 10, 20, or 30 years of retirement. That's a long time to be trying to replace income.

Now, let's take a look at pensions. We don't see them as much as we used to, but there are still many out there, especially for people who worked for the government.

Pensions usually come with two distribution options, either a monthly benefit or a lump sum. Over the years, I have seen more and more lump-sum options. I believe this is because pension providers want to reduce their future liabilities and offer lump sum options as incentives to relieve their future obligations to pay a monthly annuity benefit.

Let's look at an example I see often: As you get ready to retire, you're offered $2,000 a month or a lump sum of $480,000. If you take the lump sum option, you don't get $2,000 a month. It's an either/or situation.

If your main focus is maximizing the amount of monthly income today, oftentimes opting for the monthly pension benefit makes more sense.

However, if you don't necessarily need the income right away – or would like to have some flexibility or control over that money – then, it's advisable to take the lump sum option instead. Making the decision comes down to understanding what your mindsets are and knowing what your cash needs are.

That said, when it comes to taking the monthly benefit, there are a few other key factors to consider:

Pension solvency: From 2008 to 2014, the projected deficit for pensions went from a $500 million deficit projection to $42 billion. I'm not suggesting your pension will become insolvent; I'm simply suggesting that there are serious problems with the viability of pensions that should be cause for concern. The overall financial health of your pension provider is definitely something to keep in mind as you choose between the lump sum and the monthly benefit options. If you opt for the monthly benefit, you become 100% reliant on the pension provider staying solvent.

Disinheriting your kids: That $2,000 a month may come to you for life, and it may even come to your spouse for life, but it will not go to your kids. If you or your spouse is receiving a benefit and you both die, the benefit stops.

Access to cash: Often, 5, 10, or 15 years into retirement, priorities change. Some of your needs may change and having access to cash, and the flexibility and control of those dollars can help you make good, solid decisions for yourself. The monthly benefit will give you little flexibility here.

The pension trap: Some pensions only give you the monthly benefit option. Often, in these situations the pension will have spousal benefits tied into them. However, if that's not the case, you may be able to take a reduced monthly benefit in which you essentially give a portion of your monthly payout back to your pension in order to ensure your spouse receives a monthly benefit after you die. However, if your spouse dies before you, you may not have anything paid out to anybody. That's the pension trap– paying for a benefit that no one ever gets to use.

Retirement planning is about having access to money when you need it and having as much control as possible to fulfill the purpose of that money. Knowing how you plan to use the money is the most important deciding factor when it comes to determining what to do with payouts coming from a 401(k) or pension.

Regaining control of the money you have accumulated in a 401(k) or pension offers a great opportunity to put that money to work for you throughout your retirement. In the following sections, I'll suggest options for how you can achieve that.

Annuities

When it comes to planning your retirement, there's a lot you can't control. For example, you can't control the market, how long you're going to live, inflation, health care costs, your health care needs, tax law changes, pension or Social Security solvency, economic shifts, government intervention… the list goes on.

All this uncertainty surrounding retirement is actually why annuities are so popular. They are a way to transfer risk over to an insurance company so we can rely on them to cover losses when things outside of our control occur.

Whether or not you should use an annuity depends entirely on your unique situation.

That is not a popular stance to have, since those who sell annuities suggest that everyone should own an annuity, while those who sell investments tend to badmouth them. Whether you promote an annuity should not be based on your business model, but on what is best for the client. With that in mind, it's easy to see why people have been confused about whether buying an annuity is appropriate for them.

When it comes to who may be a candidate for annuities, here's how I see it:

- **Consider saying yes to annuities:** If you are someone approaching retirement who wants to grow and protect your retirement income or who simply wants to keep some of your money out of the market, protected from downside risk, then look into annuities.

- **Consider saying no to annuities:** If you don't fall into one of these two camps, then it is likely that an annuity isn't the best option for you. There are a few other special uses, but that is a whole other discussion.

In addition to the lack of communication by insurance and investment advisors, there are also several common myths about annuities that can make them sound less appealing. Here are the ones I hear the most:

- **Annuities have lower growth potential.** The truth is that some annuities can grow just as competitively as a regularly managed portfolio.

- **An income annuity will run out of money.** The truth is that while, yes, an annuity can run out of money, an investment portfolio carries the same risk of running out of money… only without the insurance.

- **Annuities are too expensive.** The truth is that some annuities can be pretty expensive when you add together all the rider options and contract fees, but what is often not mentioned is that some annuities have no fees at all.

- **The stock market has historically performed well enough that there is no need for the guarantees of an annuity.** We don't know for sure what the future holds, but when people discuss historical performance, I find that their references are often too short-sighted to understand the reality over time. This is where sequence of return risk to a portfolio over a reasonable time frame can help provide perspective.

For example, if you were to retire in 1989 and enjoyed the bull run of the 1990s then experienced the reversal of good fortune in the 2000s, you would have seen the best and the worst of the market. It illustrates that markets will move with earnings and headlines, but economic and political cycles are the real drivers of the market and the long-tailed effects are what can propel you or sink you.

Sequence of Returns Comparison

Year	Total Return	Balance		Year	Total Return	Balance
1989	31.69%	1,266,900	1	2008	-37.00%	580,000
1990	-3.11%	1,175,999	2	2007	5.49%	560,342
1991	30.47%	1,481,281	3	2006	15.79%	595,775
1992	7.62%	1,539,519	4	2005	4.91%	570,391
1993	10.08%	1,638,427	5	2004	10.88%	576,174
1994	1.32%	1,602,090	6	2003	28.68%	683,457
1995	37.58%	2,144,453	7	2002	-22.10%	472,711
1996	22.96%	2,575,326	8	2001	-11.89%	355,012
1997	33.36%	3,371,116	9	2000	-9.11%	259,332
1998	28.58%	4,269,343	10	1999	21.04%	248,656
1999	21.04%	5,100,416	11	1998	28.58%	252,527
2000	-9.11%	4,566,557	12	1997	33.36%	267,558
2001	-11.89%	3,952,305	13	1996	22.96%	257,701
2002	-22.10%	3,005,419	14	1995	37.58%	281,118
2003	28.68%	3,791,744	15	1994	1.32%	209,199
2004	10.88%	4,126,387	16	1993	10.08%	152,388
2005	4.91%	4,248,757	17	1992	7.62%	83,765
2006	15.79%	4,836,994	18	1991	30.47%	26,646
2007	5.49%	5,017,423	19	1990	-3.11%	0
2008	-37.00%	3,073,301	20	1989	31.69%	0
Avg:	10.36%			Avg:	10.36%	

Starting value of $1 million earning S&P 500 historic annual returns
with annual withdrawals of $50,000 indexed for 3% inflation. Past
performance is no guarantee of future results.

Above is an example of a 20-year time frame
side by side with the returns reversed, assuming
a $1 million balance at the beginning with a
$50,000 annual withdrawal rate and a 3%
inflation factor.

As you can see, the left side grows while the right side runs out of money with the exact same average return. This is called the sequence of return risk, and it adds to the complexities of retirement income planning while relying on the stock market. It is not the returns that matter as much as the sequence of those returns.

In the end, whether you use an annuity or not is less important than understanding why you're making the decision. Just remember to rely only on the circumstances you can control and to use the best information available.

After all, no one loves insurance unless they find themselves using it to replace something valuable that they lost. At that point, they are always thankful they have it.

Life Insurance

When it comes to constructing a portfolio, we know that diversification through asset allocation is the ultimate goal and an attempt to control risk. That's why you might want to consider using life insurance as an asset class in your portfolio. Let's talk about what that means.

When used and designed properly, life insurance is a very effective tool with a multitude of practical applications. When most people think of life insurance, they think of protection for families and pensions and business liabilities. But there are plenty of other, less common uses for life insurance, including banking, retirement tax reduction, long-term care funding, and portfolio diversification.

As far as I can tell, there are two basic reasons life insurance isn't commonly considered when it comes to these alternative uses:

1. Life insurance is complex.

2. Life insurance plans are cloaked in negativity.

When I started out in the financial business in 1993, I started by selling life insurance – and I absolutely hated it. I spent a couple of years learning the insurance business then jumped to investments as soon as I could. I just didn't like how it was being packaged and sold to people. That is a problem that still exists today.

However, as I got more and more involved in financial planning, I realized that there was a real need for life insurance. I still incorporate it into my practice. I just approach it in an entirely different way.

So, before we go any further, I need you to forget everything you've heard about life insurance – at least temporarily. Any preconceived notions you have about life insurance will likely overshadow the information I am sharing with you here, so it's important to set aside any bias you may have.

The most common plan I use is a specially-designed life insurance (SDLI) contract. Basically, it's a dividend-paying whole life insurance policy with a high cash value.

Why whole life? Well, this type of policy can be considered property. Once you fund it for a specific period of time, you own it. There are no future payment obligations, and the benefit and cash value are yours.

All other forms of life insurance, such as universal life, index life, and variable life, are perpetual-payment designs. In other words, the payments never end, whether the policy owner makes the payment or the premiums are deducted from the cash value of the contract.

When whole life insurance is used as an asset class, these plans also allow for a tax-free death benefit, tax-free growth of cash, and (if handled properly) tax-free access to cash.

For instance, one challenge savers face is the necessity for holding cash in low-yield savings accounts in order to have easy access to those funds. The trade-off for that easy access is little to no growth on their assets. Furthermore, while bank accounts offer a safe place to store cash, yields are low and are taxable.

On the other hand, a well-designed SDLI can rival a bank savings account due to its high, early cash values. While viewed mostly as a longer term financial vehicle, SDLIs offer access to the account by allowing you to surrender value through policy loans or withdrawals. Their earnings are in line with bond yields at 3-4% and are treated favorably by the IRS for tax purposes. They also offer an enhanced death benefit and some long-term care benefits.

Of course, life insurance is just one piece of your (much bigger) financial picture. When it comes to diversifying your assets and controlling your risk, it could be a valuable tool for the right person.

Investing Like Yale

When it comes to investing, for decades and decades, the average investor has been made a promise: If they fund their retirement accounts, pay off their home quickly, and store money in the bank, security will follow.

But, while the average person is focused almost solely on rapidly paying down debt, they are finding that home repairs, college tuition, and automobile purchases all compete for the same resources. Furthermore, storing cash in the bank doesn't do anything to grow their money for the future.

Since most of the average person's investments are tied directly to the stock market, market extremes only intensify the issues. When markets are good, greed sets in and there is euphoria, optimism, and hope. It's equivalent to a gambler's rush. When markets are bad, fear sets in and there is anxiety, pessimism and hopelessness.

I hope by explaining the different options for using your money listed in this chapter, I've shown you that there's a better way, but as further proof, let's take a look at Yale's endowment. Now you may be asking why you would compare yourself to a multibillion-dollar endowment, but the answer is simple. Your goals are the same: to create consistent streams of income.

The number one thing large investors like Yale realize is that income is king. Financial freedom, security, and success are not determined solely by how much money you have. They know what's really important is how much income is generated from the assets you do have.

The second thing the wealthiest investors understand is that you can't leave your finances to chance by relying on markets alone in your search for yield. Because they are focused on generating income, they do not rely on 401(k)s, average rates of return, and stock market performance to find security for themselves or reach new levels of financial independence.

Per their website, Yale's aim is a diverse portfolio that heavily favors "non-traditional" asset classes. They use proven strategies to generate consistent streams of income with a focus on avoiding losses – all with only 17% in the stock market.

This approach is radically different to that of the average 401(k) investor, who allocates nearly 100% of their assets and contributions to domestic and foreign equity mutual funds.

While the average investor is unlikely to have direct access to the same opportunities that a multibillion-dollar endowment has, there are alternative investment opportunities that can be used to mirror Yale's approach: non-traditional real estate, private equity and hedge funds, natural resources, and managed futures. It's really just a matter of finding a financial adviser who understands and has access to these types of opportunities.

To sum it up: Yale uses their assets to generate income to fund their operations, just like you should be using your investments to generate income to support your lifestyle. And that is the key difference between how the most successful investors think, versus how the average person thinks.

The Silent Killer: Inflation

One of the main enemies of retirement is inflation. It's known as the "silent killer" because it results in the slow deterioration of the purchasing power of your money. Inflation pushes the prices of goods and services up, requiring you to earn more money to maintain the same lifestyle. It impacts your life in small doses, which makes it easily overlooked from one year to the next, but its effects can be problematic long-term.

The remedy for protecting your investments and saving your accounts from inflation is straightforward and involves following some simple math. If you earn 2% on a bank CD, and inflation is running at 2%, you have broken even. You would not have earned or lost any money. However, there are taxes due on the 2% in earnings, which results in a net loss. It's not enough to keep up with inflation; you must earn more than the anticipated rate of inflation and taxes combined.

When it comes to retirement planning, inflation can leave you with a false sense of how much you will need in the future. An inflation rate of 2% might seem like a small figure, but when you multiply it over ten years, it translates to 20% or 20 cents on a dollar. In other words, with a compounding inflation rate of 2%, if you require $50,000 today, you'll need $59,754 in 10 years to live an equivalent lifestyle.

So, if you require $50,000 today in 20 years, you would need to have $72,840 of income to live the same lifestyle.

Inflation can be a difficult concept to wrap your mind around. The effects of it are obvious, but planning for it can sometimes be a challenge because the future is unpredictable.

In the remainder of this chapter, I'll explain how inflation begins and why it happens. This will help you to form a basic understanding of pricing of goods and services, our government, the Federal Reserve, and business operations. It will help clarify many misunderstandings of how our economy works and provide you with an appreciation for how intertwined elements of the system really are.

Supply and Demand

If you have ever experienced the desire or the need for something that was in short supply, you likely recall the fact that the item was difficult to find. Other people wanted and were buying the same thing you wanted, making the availability of the item limited. Often, when you have an item that is in high demand and there is a limited supply of the item, retailers and manufacturers will increase the price of the item to capitalize on the situation.

However, there is often a balance of supply and demand which stabilizes prices. A company is not going to intentionally produce more of a product than what they believe they can sell, and if the demand is high, they will produce more to satisfy the demand.

An example of how this works is with the world's oil supply. Oil is something that is in high demand since most of us need to fuel our vehicles. When we fill up our gas tanks, this triggers a need for more oil to be produced for the next person to fill up. The amount of oil pumped out of the ground to manufacture gasoline is regulated up or down based on how much gasoline is being used. The oil is extracted from the ground and distributed into the market at a high enough level to satisfy the need, but it is kept at a low enough level to keep prices stable. Being that there is such a high demand for fuel, a sudden shortage of fuel would surely cause the price of a gallon of gas to soar.

(A couple of facts about oil are that it is highly political, and it plays a significant role in our world's economics. Since oil is traded globally using American dollars, the exchange rate of our currency with an oil producing country is a contributing factor in the price of a gallon of gas. As the dollar declines and the exchange rate widens, the price of gas goes up. This is an origination point of inflation leading to people having less money to spend on other things, which in turn has a negative impact on the economy.)

Now, imagine for a moment that you have a small business that requires the transport of widgets from one location to another. If there is an increase in the price of a gallon of gas, your fuel costs rise causing an increase in your transportation costs. To avoid losing money, you are forced to combat this increase by reducing your expenses and increasing revenue. This is accomplished by cutting jobs, closing facilities, and increasing the price of your widgets.

The effect of this is an increase in the cost for consumers to purchase the widget which in turn forces people to reduce other household expenses. Now, people are spending less money on goods and services which leads to companies not selling enough of their product and forces those companies to cut more jobs and raise their prices. The effects are a never-ending spiral of job losses and price increases. When this begins to happen, the government intervenes.

Government

I read a book written by L. Carlos Lara and Robert P. Murphy titled, *How Privatized Banking Really Works,* which does a great job explaining the banking system of the United States. In the book, the authors used the example of the former Roman Empire to explain the impact inflation and the devaluation of currency has on an economy. The book illustrates the destructive patterns of government and the influence they have on our daily lives.

In the book, the authors used the example of Caesar who was the ruler of the former Roman Empire. I will summarize their point here by saying that Caesar was a man that was known for overindulgence and power. The key to his success was his military, which he used to conquer neighboring territories to strip them of their assets coupled with the enforcement of collecting taxes from the people. The acquired wealth along with the taxes collected was used to pay for the expansion and the funding of his military, architecture, and infrastructure.

Over time, Caesar found himself in a situation where he was not collecting enough gold from the people of Rome to pay for the needs and expenses he had to keep his empire running. So, he had a choice to make, cut spending or reduce the size of his government. Well, he did not want to do either so he decided that he would keep doing what he was doing and would pay for his expenses by creating more money.

Caesar shaved his gold coins in order to produce additional coins, which he then used to pay for goods and services. He manipulated the currency being used for commerce within his kingdom and attempted to pass off the counterfeit coins as being the same as before. The result was an increase in his bank account which enabled him to continue to operate without cutting expenses. However, this did backfire on him when the merchants were handed the new coins for goods and services and noticed that the coins were smaller. In response to the lighter coins, the merchants demanded two coins for the same goods and services.

As time went on, Caesar was faced with yet another deficit spending year and responded in the same manner. He attempted to counterfeit the coins again, but the merchants responded by adding safety features to the coins to easily detect if the coins were altered. Now that he was unable to reduce the size of the coins, Caesar decided to melt all the coins down to then reproduce them using a combination of gold and another metal to create more coins. Caesar continued this process until the coins ultimately contained less than one percent gold deeming the money worthless. Well, we all know what happened to Rome and, unfortunately, our modern day government is repeating the errors of the Romans by spending at unsustainable levels.

The United States of America once used physical gold and silver as currency then adopted the use of a paper certificate replacing physical gold for ease of transporting currency. The certificate guaranteed that there was gold somewhere to support its value. In the meantime, our government incrementally reduced the content of silver in our coins until ultimately removing the precious metal altogether. Then finally the government removed the gold standard which debased our money from the value of gold.

The money we now use is called fiat money or in other words, money made out of thin air. It is a form of currency that governments from around the world issue and control its value so they can fund their obligations. The way this works is that if the government needs more money, they have the ability to have more created. Since the government seems to continually need more and more money, they seem to have more and more created. This process devalues our currency, spurring inflation.

Earlier I discussed how rising gasoline prices can create a ripple effect ultimately leading to inflation and job losses. These are contributing factors to government involvement since a reduction of income and spending reduces the amount of taxes it collects. Now, you would think the government would cut back on its spending just as you and I would if its income was reduced, but that is not exactly how our government operates. You would also think that the easy solution to this is to raise taxes (which our government does regularly, directly and indirectly), but it also knows that it can only tax the population so much before there is a revolt. There is a limit to what it can force us to pay without creating more problems leaving it holding the proverbial bag and unable to cover its obligations. So, just as Caesar did, it creates more money by literally making more currency.

The Fed's Role

How does this process work? Well, it's difficult to explain, but essentially, the government issues an I.O.U to the Federal Reserve Bank similar to how you would go and borrow money from the bank to buy something. They make a promise to the Federal Reserve to repay the money with interest. The Federal Reserve then lends the money to our government who uses the money to pay its bills. This process floods the economy with new money (benefiting the government) which causes the dollars already in circulation to be worthless due to having too much money in circulation, similar to the effects of Caesar's actions in ancient Rome.

The key takeaway from this is that the Federal Reserve creates money out of thin air to pass it on to the government. This is what we have heard about in recent years under the name of "Stimulus" or "Quantitative Easing." There is also something called Fractional Reserve Banking that floods the economy with money every day.

Remember what happened when Caesar flooded the market with manipulated coins? The merchants, in turn, demanded more of the coins for the same goods and services. This is what happens in modern times as well, but we have to think on a global scale.

Goods and services, including oil, are traded around the world. The exchange rate between one currency to another is in part how inflation can seep into the system. If we are buying oil from Saudi Arabia, their rival's exchange rate for our dollar may be low, forcing them to charge more for the oil. This is the same for gold and silver as well. As the dollar goes down in value, the value of gold and silver along with other precious metals tends to rise. It is all about conversion rates, supply and demand, and government actions.

Though simplified (but still complicated), these are a few of the components for how inflation is created. The challenge of inflation is not something to focus on since you have limited control of how it is created.

However, being aware of it enables you to combat the erosion of the purchasing power of your money. This means saving more money to get to retirement and to sustain your lifestyle throughout retirement.

Managing Cash Flow

Think of your personal financial situation as a puzzle with dozens of pieces, each representing a product, program, idea, thought, decision, purchase, or investment that impacts your overall financial plan. The picture on the puzzle's box is your cash flow. Understanding it helps you focus on where your money needs to go to fulfill the goals you have for your future.

Every financial move you make originates with cash flow. You simply cannot put the puzzle together without it, which makes it the most important aspect of planning to understand. However, far too many new retirees aren't focused on cash flow and are instead concerned only with making sure they don't run out of money. But if your focus is always on "not running out of money in retirement," you will live a very frugal and poor retirement lifestyle. As the saying goes, you'll be playing not to lose rather than playing to win.

When you, instead, take steps to optimize your cash flow by keeping control of more of your money while creating passive income streams, you can change your mindset from avoiding running out of money to thinking about retirement as the next chapter in your life. A chapter where you are both growing and protecting your wealth so that you can experience true financial freedom.

Let's get you focused on winning in retirement and doing things differently.

What is Cash Flow?

To start, I think it's important to know the basics of cash flow. Essentially, cash flow is understanding where your money originates. It's about strategically using money to not only live your life but to create more income sources for yourself. When you put your focus on cash flow, it solves a hundred other problems. The purpose of cash flow awareness is not simply to make ends meet, but rather to properly organize the flow of money, which allows you to create wealth and avoid debt.

Employment or a business may fund your cash flow, or it can be income generated from your assets. Regardless of its source, you have cash flowing through your hands, and it is either flowing out of your control or into your control via three primary areas: reoccurring obligations, irregular obligations, and savings (storage).

1. Reoccurring obligations are financial transactions that occur on a regular basis, often considered part of a budget. A mortgage payment, for example.

2. Irregular obligations are financial transactions that occur less frequently but would be part of your planned expenses throughout a calendar year. These might include your yearly tax liabilities.

3. Savings are the amount of money over and above your obligations that you do not need now but will store for a future purpose.

Having a working knowledge of your cash flow helps you establish flexibility, access, and control of your money, which can allow you to retain and utilize more money during your lifetime and for future generations.

The sooner you identify what money is flowing *out* of your control to banks, the government, or other third parties, the sooner you can have more money flowing *into* your control.

Everything is about cash flow! Once you understand the reasons you are losing control of your money through things like mortgage payments or tax liabilities, you can begin to take back control of your money and your financial life.

How to Solve for Better Cash Flow

When you retire, you might be tempted to use money you have invested to make needed home improvements or even to pay down your mortgage. And conventional wisdom would probably even tell you those are sound financial decisions. After all, by using money you have invested to make home improvements, you could avoid going into debt while getting the home upgrades you want. And by paying off your mortgage, you'd no longer have a monthly mortgage payment and could save that amount each month.

But I challenge you to instead think about how you could be using those funds to turn them into future income. Everything, especially in retirement when you're no longer working, is about income...how your cash is flowing and working for you needs to be the focus.

For instance, many Financial Entertainers use catch phrases such as "Debt is Bad"..."Live Debt Free"..."You shouldn't have any debt"..."Pay off your house"...etc. And while this may seem to be sound financial advice on the surface, it can restrict you from getting the most from your resources. This idea goes against what the wealthy do and think, which is "how can I can use other people's money to increase my assets and cash flow?"

This is a hidden lever the wealthy use to generate more monthly income. An example of this is a client I helped recently who wanted to use $150,000 of their investments to remodel their home. However, their investments were producing around $9,000 per year of income for them, which would have stopped if they used the money to do their renovations.

They were on the back side of their mortgage with a balance of $25,000 and a monthly mortgage payment of $970. I asked them whether their home would appreciate in value any less if they had a bigger mortgage, and of course, the answer was no.

I pointed out that since the home would appreciate the same either way that the equity in the home is a dead asset...it's not doing anything for them. I suggested using that dead asset to complete the renovations, which would actually increase the value of the home itself without requiring them to use any of their investments. Their mortgage went from $25,000 to $175,000 while reducing their mortgage payment by $2,200/year and maintaining their investment income of $9,000/year.

By not following the so-called expert advice, they were able to lower their cash needs and now have their renovations done along with $11,200/year in cash flow. If they would have followed conventional advice, they would have left $11,200 of income on the table, giving it up for the rest of their life.

This is just one powerful tool for increasing cash flow. There are many more I use to help increase income. Remember, we always want to be thinking about how we are going to create the most income from the resources that you have so you can live the life you want. More on how to do that in the next section.

Passive Income: The True Key to Financial Freedom

I talk to people all the time who have accumulated a significant amount of money in their retirement accounts. They've followed the standard advice of saving for retirement to accumulate money for their future. Yet, when they want to retire, they look at their stack of money and don't know what to do. They have the money, but the money isn't giving them what they need.

Average investors have been promised that if they fund their retirement accounts, accelerate the payoff on their home, and store money in the bank, then security will follow. But for most, that never happens.

True financial freedom isn't reached by chasing returns or parking money in a bank or retirement account. It requires having a consistent flow of passive income to fund the life you want to live without having to work to earn a paycheck. The responsibility of producing income shifts away from you having to trade your time for money to your assets creating passive income.

So, how does one do that? First, stop believing the lies you've been told about money your whole life. One of the lies many people believe is that the stock market will always go up over time and that if you take from your stack of money the stock market will replace what was taken. This is a fairly ridiculous concept considering the fact that the stock market doesn't always go up. There are times when it goes down. There are also times when it's flat or returns very little.

As I described in the investing chapter, endowments like Yale's grow their wealth by having less exposure to traditional investments and are focused on income producing strategies with the goal of achieving consistent cash flow.

You also have to stop believing the lie that what's really best for your money is to hold onto it for dear life by essentially burying it in the backyard. It's hard to imagine this as a viable income strategy unless you believe the money itself is financial independence. But the reality is eventually you'll need some of that buried money so you'll dig it up, taking from your stack, making it smaller, and in turn, diminishing the independence you thought you had.

It's time to adopt the mindset that the ultra-wealthy have understood all along. What successful people have figured out is the importance of putting their money to work for them to create consistent income. The wealthy follow a system, a roadmap of sorts for creating income that supplies their financial freedom.

If you have successfully accumulated money in your bank, investment, and retirement accounts, you need to understand that you're only halfway there. There is still work to be done. You have to take the money you have and create predictable streams of income that will keep cash flowing for you until you reach financial freedom.

Anatomy of a Retirement Plan

Throughout the retirement preparation process, there will be times when you feel as though you are making a series of rapid-fire micro decisions as you work through Social Security benefits, Medicare options, pension elections, and retirement account distributions.

The decisions to be made are many, and understanding the long-term ramifications of those decisions is paramount, considering that your retirement years could be as many as those spent working.

The numerous options you will face can become a labyrinth of choices leading many people to attend "YouTube University" in search of answers, while leaning on friends and co-workers to fill in the missing pieces. The truth is, people underestimate the complexities that exist with preparing for retirement and find themselves over their head.

Unfortunately, without understanding the long-term effects of one decision over another, a retiree may be well into their retirement before problems begin to surface. For instance,

- Inflation will erode your income over time.

- Longevity may require your money to last longer than you thought.

- Market volatility can deplete your resources.

- Health care expenses can potentially absorb most of what you have.

- Taxes can absorb a third of your income.

By the time these risks are exposed, retirees find themselves stuck. That is why retirement planning shouldn't be viewed as a rapid-fire micro decision-making process but rather a time to design a master plan focused on what you can control and protecting yourself from what you can't.

Think of it like building a home ... you wouldn't begin construction without first having blueprints drawn up. Your retirement plan is the blueprint for your retirement, while

Social Security benefits, Medicare options, pension elections and retirement account distributions are your building materials.

Planning for a Sustainable Retirement

Continuing with the home construction metaphor, to ensure you have your bases covered and are retirement ready, first consider the cost of the project. It is better to estimate the cost of your retirement now to uncover potential problems before actually retiring. Start by carefully evaluating your current retirement readiness by filling out the Successful Retirement Checklist. You can download it here: **brianskrobonja.com/retirement-checklist** Then, read on for more guidance on how to think through your situation.

1. Develop an income plan detailing exactly how much income you will need each year to fund your retirement lifestyle.

Now, before skipping over this, you should consider that your lifestyle will change — along with your tax situation — which means that the amount you now need to live on will not be the same when you retire. You may need to budget even more for your early years of retirement, when you'll be enjoying the good life. So, it is not a good idea to make general assumptions about your future income needs based on how things are while you're working.

Carefully consider what will change and what will stay the same once you retire, adding into the mix such things as travel, health care costs, and other variable expenses.

2. Identify your income sources and determine exactly how much income will be generated from each source to satisfy your annual income needs.

No generalizations here … you should seek to know exactly how much you can expect from each resource you have.

This is where most people begin to struggle, because there is often a disconnect between their mindset around their assets and the need they have from them. There are generally two camps with this:

- Those who focus on protecting their principal by holding cash.

- And others who hold on to their investment portfolios in hopes for long-term growth.

Both camps are focused on growing or preserving their money, making it difficult for them to adjust for their need to receive consistent income from the assets.

3. Map your assets out and separate them by their purpose.

What I find is that most people have money sitting in bank accounts, large amounts of equity in their home and money combined together in their investment portfolios.

And while this may seem an ideal arrangement, it is important to point out that cash in the bank is not earning anything, equity in a home is not earning anything, and money in the stock market has varying levels of risk … none of which translates to having consistent income in retirement.

In most instances, the assets you have are either going to be spent or used for income now or in the future.

So, a good place to begin would be identifying which assets fall into these categories.

4. Have an income replacement plan in place for your spouse to cover the loss of Social Security or pension income if you were to predecease them.

Developing an income strategy for retirement most often means you are relying on a husband and wife's benefits, but those benefits are only received while both are living (in most cases).

Many people are misled into believing that as you get older your need for life insurance diminishes, and while this may be true for some, for others the need for it may actually rise.

It is a good idea to know the specifics for how benefits will adjust when a death occurs and have a plan in place to replace lost income if it is needed.

5. Have (updated) legal documents in place designating financial power of attorney, medical directives, wills and trusts.

Most people kick this can down the road with the idea they will have time to get this done later. (Later meaning when they need it.)

Here is the deal: If you wait until you need these documents it will be too late to get them.

6. Have a contingency plan in place to cover health care costs if you were to find yourself needing long-term nursing care.

This is an area that so many people ignore, crossing their fingers and hoping nothing happens to them that would require this level of care. However, considering the cost of nursing care, it is not something to ignore. You need to know how this cost will be covered if you find yourself needing care.

The cheapest way to cover this risk is through insurance, but some may choose to spend down a portion of their assets to cover the costs. Either way, it is a good idea to have this mapped out and know how you plan to cover the cost if incurred.

Using these steps as your retirement planning blueprint you can begin to establish a strong foundation for a happy retirement.

A Retirement Savings Portfolio Focused on Financial Freedom

As I touched on in Steps 2 and 3 of the previous section, there's often a disconnect between what people say they want in retirement – i.e. financial security – and how they're actually managing their assets – i.e. storing money in a bank, putting money away in a tax-deferred account, and paying off their mortgage.

The reality is those methods will bring underwhelming, mostly frustrating results. Why? Because:

- If you are storing money at the bank, the bank is making money on your money while paying you next to nothing in return.

- If you are borrowing money from the bank, you are giving up control of a portion of your cash flow to repay the loan while paying the bank interest.

- And when you fund a tax-deferred account, you're allowing the government to dictate when you can access your money – and they will have to let you know later what tax rate you will pay them since they don't know what taxes will be in the future.

- When it comes to mortgage payoff acceleration, it is a race to zero with no wealth creation and no access to cash.

As you plan for your retirement, you can settle for the status quo, or you can think outside the box and do something different. As I mentioned, what most savers are looking for is financial security. I define financial security as having access to cash when you need it for the rest of your life. This is easier said than done, of course, but it is where we need to begin.

There are four broad categories to consider when looking for products to accomplish this goal: long-term growth, consistent income, access to cash, and tax mitigation.

Long-Term Growth

Aside from entrepreneurship and real estate, public stock markets have the highest growth potential over the long term. But there are two other aspects to growth that savers often overlook: growth through income and the idea of uninterrupted growth.

Growth through income centers around an asset creating income to reinvest, and it is best achieved through private markets, such as real estate, private equity and private debt. There is simply too much volatility in public markets to effectively pursue a growth through income strategy. It can be done but not as effectively.

Uninterrupted growth has more to do with how money is flowing. Let me explain: When you spend money, that money is gone and no longer working for you. However, using a private banking strategy that capitalizes on the unique features of a whole life insurance policy, you can actually have money accumulating in the contract while borrowing money to make your purchases. This leveraging strategy keeps your money growing uninterrupted while accessing money through loans collateralized by the contract. In other words, you're building wealth on money you would otherwise spend. This is one of the most underutilized strategies because most people (including insurance agents who sell insurance) don't understand how it works.

One other thing about the insurance design … the money grows and is accessible tax-free without age restrictions. This is a big deal as you will see in a moment.

Stacking these three growth strategies together expands your diversification, reduces risk, reduces volatility and can increase your wealth more efficiently and with more control.

Consistent Income

Having consistent income ranks highest on the list of things needed to have financial security and is the primary reason traditional investments in the public stock market held inside or outside of traditional retirement accounts are less likely to be used for this purpose.

Without consistent income flowing into your checking account, you cannot effectively manage your cash flow, and if the source of that income is at risk of losing value, you add another layer of insecurity about the longevity of your income. This is a huge revelation for people, considering that the public stock market is the status quo default in retirement plans and is the least manageable of all ideas being discussed.

You cannot control the markets and therefore cannot predict the income, account value or its longevity. It's all hypothetical to assume what stock markets will do, but supporting your cash flow needs for 30 years in retirement is not hypothetical … it's real, and there is little margin for error.

Annuities and private market investments are best suited for income and should be the primary source for fulfilling the goal of having consistent income. You just need to know how to solve for this effectively.

Access to Cash

Having access to cash is also high on the list for financial security and is another reason traditional investment in the public stock market held inside or outside of traditional retirement accounts is not the best option for holding cash. Age restrictions, market volatility and tax liabilities are all downsides of these products, making them problematic for storing cash.

Bank accounts are another default option for storing cash, but these accounts earn close to nothing and are taxable. Those two reasons alone are motivation to find an alternative.

Again, public markets are best suited for long-term growth, and banks are best used for moving money around to pay your bills and conduct business. They are not best suited for holding cash.

A specially designed whole life insurance contract as previously mentioned is much better suited for storing cash with tax-free growth, tax-free access, consistent growth and no government age restrictions.

Tax Mitigation

Everyone desires tax mitigation, but it is mostly heard about and seldom seen in real life. The reason is simple: These strategies fall outside the status quo. People mistakenly think tax deferral is a tax mitigation method, but in actuality it is the primary source of tax problems in retirement.

It is a paradox that people who defer taxes with 401(k)s, IRAs and other similar retirement accounts think they are saving on taxes – because they are actually causing a larger tax problem for themselves. True tax saving is not tax deferral. Tax deferral just kicks the can down the road.

If you are already in a situation where you have a large amount of money in tax-deferred accounts and are looking for strategies to convert taxable assets to tax-free, then you will want to work with a team of experts who can help guide you through what is being discussed here.

The Family Office Model

The work and planning involved in creating a retirement plan and pursuing investment strategies that will provide you with financial security might seem overwhelming. The good news is that you don't need to do it all on your own, and in fact, the super wealthy don't...

I want to share a concept that you may have never heard about, even though it has been around for more than 100 years. It's called a Family Office. The concept of family offices was pioneered by John D. Rockefeller when he formed one of the first known family offices in 1882. His goal in creating this model was to protect and grow his wealth while putting a wealth-creation system in place that could function for generations.

What ultra-wealthy families like the Rockefellers have figured out that I believe others have not is that using a family office model gives them a definite advantage by facilitating access to teams of investment, tax, and insurance professionals along with attorneys and financial planners to guide them through their financial decisions. This is an advantage of both time and talent that frees them from the enormous responsibility of managing wealth on their own.

Having an integrated team of professionals all working synergistically together can bring vastly greater overall results and is why the ultra-wealthy have viewed these teams as a necessary investment and necessity for more than a century.

The ultra-wealthy realize that they can't possibly know everything, which contributes to their wealth and is why they surround themselves with smart people to support and make decisions for them, which frees them to not have to become an expert in such things as cash flow, investments, insurance law, and real estate.

Money, wealth, success, and legacies take effort to create and maintain. Successful people understand the importance of acquiring and developing the right relationships to help them reach new levels. It often requires the right mindset of wanting more for yourself and committing to doing things differently than the average person.

A family office is about complete financial management–from cash flow to taxes. It includes estate planning and income planning. It's about legacy and generational planning. It includes making big-ticket purchases and utilizing good debt management. It involves sound insurance choices and protecting assets.

Unfortunately, due to the exorbitant payroll cost and complexities around maintaining such a team, family offices have necessarily been reserved for the ultra-wealthy. Until now. I've developed an integrated multi-family office model, which operates as a traditional family office while serving multiple families instead of just a single family. This system brings an experienced team of professionals to the table to coordinate resources, help manage cash flow, help reduce taxes, get a generational estate plan in place, offer holistic asset management and insurance planning to those who desire that level of support. The only difference is that this team serves several families instead of a single family.

Think about what it would feel like to have a family office for yourself. The feeling of having a comprehensive plan in place, not questioning whether you've missed something in your planning and knowing you have a team of people working for you, removing the responsibility of having to figure everything out on your own.

Imagine having your taxes prepared by a tax professional who actually helped with developing a tax strategy specifically for your situation. Imagine having a chronologically mapped out cash flow strategy that accounted for all large purchases and cash needs with no bank loans while continuing to grow your wealth. Imagine having an income plan in place that's designed to increase your cash flow and allows for more wealth creation and entrepreneurial opportunities while keeping control of your assets. Imagine having a network of professionals who are all collaborating to better serve you and who are available for regular meetings to review and answer your questions as they arise. That's what the family office model offers.

Wherever you are in your thinking, there is an opportunity to improve your probability for a successful retirement. To get started, figure out where you are, know where you're going, identify what obstacles stand in your way, and then, put a great team together to help you overcome them. If you wish to learn whether what the ultra-wealthy are doing can work for you, complete the Family Office Quiz at **TakeBriansQuiz.com** to see if you qualify.

Social Security

I am often asked about how to maximize social security. And let me say that there is a lot of conflicting information out there about how to utilize both these important resources.

I want to debunk some myths about social security and share some of the mistakes I see people make when they claim their benefits.

The first thing that's important to understand about social security is that it's an income replacement system. It isn't meant to be your sole source of retirement. It's set up to replace *part* of your income.

Another thing that is important to understand is that it favors low income earners. For example, a low wage earner might get 53% of their former salary through social security benefits while a high wage earner might get only 35% of their former salary through social security benefits. But that said, no matter who you are, your social security isn't going to replace a large portion of your pre-retirement income. That's why it's so important to have other income generation methods as part of your retirement plan.

There are essentially three common ages when people decide to start receiving their social security benefit:

- Age 62, because this is the youngest age at which you can begin receiving your social security benefit. However, know that your benefit will be reduced if started this early!

- Age 65, because this is also when Medicare begins.

- At full retirement age (FRA), because this is when you can get your full social security benefit. At your FRA, you can also work and earn a full income without dealing with the earnings limit that is put in place if you retire before your FRA.

The Social Security Administration (SSA) determines your FRA based on the year you were born. For anyone born between 1943 and 1954, their FRA is 66. For those born in 1955, their FRA is 66 and two months. Then, FRA goes up to 66 and four months for those born in 1956, 66 and six months for those born in 1957, 66 and eight months for those born in 1958, and 66 and 10 months for those born in 1959. For anyone born 1960 or after, their FRA is 67.

The process the SSA uses to calculate your monthly benefit amount is a little convoluted, but I think it's important to have an understanding of how your benefit will be determined. First, they take 35 years of earnings. Your earnings up to age 60 are then indexed for inflation. For any years you didn't work during those 35 years, you get a zero, and those zeros count against you when benefits are calculated.

The SSA then adds up your 35 years of earnings and divides by 420, which is 35 x 12 (for the 12 months in a year), because the SSA wants to get at what your monthly benefit will be. This, then, gives you your average indexed monthly earnings (AIME). However, this is not your benefit amount. The SSA applies a formula to your AIME and this gives you your primary insurance amount (PIA), or what's more commonly known as your monthly social security benefit.

So, knowing this is how the SSA calculates your benefits, it's very beneficial to try to work and pay into the system for as many of those 35 years as possible. If you're averaging out over 35 years, and you worked only ten of those years, the other 25 years will be zeroed out, which greatly reduces your full retirement age benefit.

That brings me to a couple of questions I get asked a lot. First, are there ways to *increase* your social security benefit amount? And second, what factors will cause your social security benefit to be *reduced*?

Let's take these one at a time. Yes, there are ways to increase your benefit amount. In fact, there are three primary ways to do so:

- You can delay receiving your benefit past your full retirement age. When this happens you get what are called delayed retirement credits (DRCs). These DRCs guarantee an 8% automatic increase to your social security benefit for every year you delay up to age 70.

- There is a cost of living adjustment (COLAs). Social security payments are adjusted annually for inflation. These cost-of-living adjustments, or COLAs, are calculated using the Consumer Price Index for Urban Wage Earners and Clerical Workers. If prices don't increase, the COLA is zero. But when they do, there is a percentage increase to social security benefits.

- You can work to make up for a year where you didn't earn what the SSA considers a substantial income. In 2022, the SSA considers a substantial income to be at least $27,000 in a year. Doing this will not give you a significant increase but can increase your benefit amount by a few dollars per month.

And naturally, there are factors that will reduce your monthly benefit amount. Usually reductions in benefit amounts occur for one of these four reasons:

- You take your benefits before your full retirement age. While it's true that you can begin receiving your social security benefit as early as 62, doing so will mean a cut to your benefit amount.

- You start your benefit before your FRA but continue to work and make more than the earnings limit. In 2022, the earnings limit is $19,560. When you earn more than this amount, you have to give back some of your social security benefit, maybe even all of it.

- You have too much taxable income. Provisional income is used to determine if any or all of your social security benefit amount will be taxed federally (Some states don't tax social security benefits while others do, so be sure to know your state's policy). The SSA determines your provisional income by taking your adjusted gross income plus half of your social security benefit. For single people, there's no tax if your provisional income is less than $25,000. For married couples, that amount is

$32,000. The most you can be taxed is 85%.

This is where tax strategies come into play; you want to keep your income level below those thresholds. When we visit with people and discuss their retirement planning, we try to help them categorize their assets in a way that's tax-efficient.

- You get hit with a windfall elimination provision (WEP) or a government pension offset (GPO). WEPs and GPOs are factors government employees, such as public school teachers, police officers, firefighters, etc., have to deal with.

Let's say you're a public school teacher who worked several jobs during the summers of your college days and therefore you qualify for a social security benefit, but you've also worked 30 years in a government job that never paid into social security.

If you file for your social security benefit, it will be reduced by a WEP. While your social security benefit cannot be entirely wiped out, it can be reduced.

In most cases, it is reduced by about 50%. If you were entitled to a full retirement age social security benefit of, let's say, $500 per month, and you were getting a public school pension or a government pension, your social security benefit would probably be reduced to about $250 a month. Of course, there's always an exception: If you reached 30 years paying into the social security system, the WEP would be wiped out, but having no WEP is very unlikely for someone who is in a government job with a government pension.

Another factor that could come into play here is a GPO. GPOs apply to a government employee's attempt to get a spousal benefit after their spouse dies, and they are, unfortunately, much more devastating than WEPs. The rule is two-thirds of your non-covered pension is the offset of any attempt to get a spousal benefit.

So, for example, let's say your spouse dies and they were receiving a social security benefit of $3,000 and you get a monthly government pension of $4,500 – if you attempt to get your spouse's social security benefit as their surviving spouse, the GPO would be assessed based on taking two-thirds of your $4500 pension, which equals $3000. So, in the end, because of the GPO, you'd get nothing from your deceased spouse's benefit.

So, those are factors that could affect your own social security benefit, but another area of concern for many of my clients is how their spouse's benefits are affected or determined under certain circumstances. A big concern, obviously, is what happens for spouses who have never worked.

There are two general types of benefits: primary social security benefits and secondary (auxiliary) benefits. A primary benefit is based on your own work record, while a secondary benefit is claimed based on someone else's work record. This is what a non-working spouse would claim.

There are a few important things to know when it comes to spousal benefits:

- Someone who has never worked can't file for a spousal benefit until after the working spouse has filed for their social security benefit.

- The maximum spousal benefit is 50% of the other spouse's primary insurance amount (PIA) or what the other spouse would get at their full retirement age (FRA).

- If one spouse works to age 70 and gets DRCs, the spousal benefit will not be based on that amount. It will be based on the working spouse's social security benefit amount at their FRA.

- If the working spouse claims their benefits before their FRA and/or if the spouse claims the spousal benefit before their FRA, the amount they're eligible for will be less than if they had waited until their FRA.

If two people are married and one dies, a widow or widower benefit can be claimed off the surviving spouse, if the surviving spouse has a benefit lower than the widow or widower benefit. The surviving spouse can claim 100% of their deceased spouse's benefit. However, you can't claim your own benefit *and* the benefit of a deceased spouse. The rule is that you have to take the higher of those two amounts.

Similar to a normal spousal benefit, if a widow(er) benefit is started before that person's FRA, it will be reduced. That said, a widow(er) benefit can start as young as age 60. The least amount of the deceased spouse's benefit that would be received if the surviving spouse starts claiming benefits at age 60 would be 71.5%.

It's also important to note that a widow(er) is allowed to start their own benefit and then switch to their deceased spouse's benefit. Or vice versa. A reason you might do this is to get DRCs so that you get a higher benefit when you finally switch to your own.

It's best to work with a financial advisor who can help you navigate these different strategies, and decide ahead of time what you'll do if you or your spouse dies and there's a loss of income as a result of losing a social security benefit or pension. While the SSA can administer your benefits and provide you with basic information, they won't advise you on the most optimal financial strategies for you in these situations.

About the Author – Brian Skrobonja

Brian was born and raised in St. Louis. Brian's father migrated from Croatia to Missouri a half-century ago and married his mother, a St. Louis native. As Brian grew up, his mom and dad modeled the importance of family and having a strong work ethic. His father worked as a lab engineer at a heating and cooling manufacturing company while running a small business on the side and his mother raised two children.

As a teen, Brian dreamed of having upscale things, such as nice cars and large homes, but he had no example to follow for how to achieve those goals. While his dad worked hard, he always traded time for money. If Brian's father wanted something, he would do extra work to earn the money to go buy it. He always had to rely on his ability to work to create the cash flow to do the things he wanted to do.

Following his father's example, as a young man in his twenties, Brian found himself having to work harder to keep up with his lifestyle. He learned the hard way that the status quo for achieving wealth was broken. After doing it wrong for years, he finally had an epiphany. He realized he needed to create income-producing assets that could pay for his lifestyle. He set a goal to have all his bills paid by passive income, and he accomplished it! And that's when his focus for what he really wanted to do for his clients came into clarity.

Today, Brian is 28 years into his profession, having built a network of professionals offering tax, mortgage, insurance, legal, and investment services, and in turn, becoming a comprehensive resource for his clients.

Brian is also very proud of his family. He is 26 years into his marriage with his awesome wife, Kari. They have three children, two married with a total of four grandchildren.

Brian feels life's worthiest pursuit is for the thing's money cannot buy: building relationships, investing in others, creating memories and experiences with loved ones. He understands that the pursuit of things will never bring satisfaction. So, rather than focusing on acquiring things, his focus is on showing others how to use their money to build income-producing assets that can support their lifestyle and fund their dreams.

Brian is passionate about educating his audience by writing books, producing a podcast, writing blogs, and speaking on topics related to wealth creation, preservation and utilization. Brian is a Charter Financial Consultant CHFC® and the author of three books: "Common Sense," "Generational Planning," and "Retirement Planning." He is the host of one of FORBES Top 10 Podcasts by Financial Advisors, the "Common-Sense Financial podcast."

He has been featured on KMOX radio and 97.1 FM Talk in St. Louis, The Dave Ramsey Show, and has been interviewed by Advisors Magazine. In 2018 he received the Future 50 Company award and in 2021 received Best in Business by St. Louis Small Business Monthly, a publication which named Brian among the Best Wealth Managers in St. Louis in 2017, 2019, 2020, 2021 and 2022. He is a contributor for Kiplinger magazine, Medium, and Advisor magazine.

Skrobonja is pronounced Skrō-bone-yŭ.

How to Put a Retirement Plan in Place So You Can Live Your Life...

Over the years I have found that the most precious resource I have is time. Time with family, time living life, time serving clients, my time on earth. We only have 24 hours each day and how we use that time is what separates successful people from the average.

When it comes to needing to know or doing something, I begin my search to find someone who knows more or who is better at something than me to do it for me which frees up my time.

What I have learned from this approach over the years is that not only do I save time, I actually collapse time because by hiring a professional it gets done better and faster than I could have done on my own.

So, don't waste time and money trying to do everything you've read about here all on your own. Each day that passes is one less day you have to experience the true freedom that comes from having your assets generating income to fund your lifestyle. There is no reason to wait to get started.

Everyone desires the freedom that comes with not having to work, whether or not you ever plan to retire. Freedom and security comes from having control over your life.

Right now you have an opportunity to not only learn the strategies that the top 1% are using to grow and protect their wealth, you can actually have my team do it for you.

If you are ready to turn your retirement investments into a steady stream of income during retirement without having to rely on things outside of your control, I invite you to reach out.

But one last thing, I want to make sure you understand who this is for because the strategies we use are not for everyone...

If you are someone who is open to being coached, have $1,000,000 or more in investable assets and are over the age of 59 ½, this could be right for you. We only accept new clients who are interested in improving their situation and who want to do what is best for their future. If this sounds like you, here's what you do next:

Visit **qualifytoworkwithbrian.com** to schedule a complimentary Financial Future Assessment with my Wealth Team.

Thank you for reading. I'm looking forward to speaking with you and working with you soon.

www.ingramcontent.com/pod-product-compliance
Lightning Source LLC
Chambersburg PA
CBHW071234170526
45165CB00003B/1095